Black Shiver Moss

for Maggie

Black Shiver Moss

Graham Mort

Seren is the book imprint of
Poetry Wales Press Ltd.
57 Nolton Street, Bridgend, Wales, CF31 3AE
www.serenbooks.com
facebook.com/SerenBooks
twitter@SerenBooks

The right of Graham Mort to be identified as
the author of this work has been asserted in accordance
with the Copyright, Designs and Patents Act, 1988.

ISBN: 978-1-78172-386-9
ebook: 978-1-78172-387-6
Kindle: 978-1-78172-388-3

A CIP record for this title is available from the British Library.

The publisher acknowledges the financial assistance of the Welsh Books Council.

Cover painting: © John Colton

Printed by Airdrie Print Services Ltd.

Author Website: www.graham-mort.com

Contents

Waking in Picardy

starts with lost, intangible
    sleep; the sputter of rooks over
orchards, their flaked black grief

    ascending; a wood pigeon crooning
wet-throated under sky's
    fallen slip of apricot grey.

Then the sputtering engine
    of a wood wasp, tipsy at fallen
plums; five lizards creeping onto

    stone, redeemed from cold cracks
in the garden wall to sun spots
    where heat adores them. A

blackbird's cadenza, a
    flycatcher's figures of eight;
the mind tilted into day

    and washed with light.
Over the pond's virulent acne
    of weed house martins stutter –

tics of air's limpid integument –
    damselflies glisten, sex to sex
promiscuously winged.

A water hen scolds her chicks
    from the black/gold eyeslits of
pike sunk into green, camouflaged

    in striped, eternal patience;
their sag-belly grins hatch under
    clouded water, below the bloomed

skin of wakefulness, beneath a
    ripening day's vast dream where
the dead still reach for us.

An Old Flame

The flame whimpers, shivering
    from a cupped match – a wayward
child, a forlorn orphan, a spendthrift
    citizen of nowhere, a white slip of
oxygen, a free radical, its tongue
    lapping at rare atmospheres, mocked
by its own limbo-dancing shadow; the
    flame flickers, flees from everything,
consumes every thing: a torchlit
    carnival, a feast of flyblown wedding
meat, the constancy of charcoal; it
    bubbles from a black crust of nylon,
shrivels human skin, kindles the stink
    of scorched rock, chars roof beams,
coils from a torched car, glares from
    a fat-spitting skull, sleeps under a
hollowed log, glows under dawn wind –
    Harmattan, Sirocco, Tramuntana –
where sparks blow from it wild as
    prayers from a prophet's lips until
it bolts again, jealous, green-eyed,
    promiscuous as hate, as indifference,
as death; jinking in townships, chanting
    at barricades, roiling in tyre necklaces,
igniting breech and muzzle, howling
    bloodshot in eyes and jaws, then leaving
again: ashen in campfires, slender in the
    draught of midnight vigils, bent double,
blown westwards, a blazing tarantula
    jagging from radio masts and rigging,
its beacon bright in polythene benders;
    now drowning, now dreaming; stumbling
and rising, igniting a new language, foot-
    loose, stepping from the sea's smoke.

Ordinary

I was talking to a gang of Friesian heifers,
　　skittish in the field behind a hawthorn hedge
when clouds seemed to lower themselves
　　and rain slanted in over the river from the
west. It was June and there was some litter
　　in the ditch and I got under a beech tree in
full leaf, then an ash, then a horse chestnut –
　　best of all – the conkers still tightly balled,
the leaves glossy-dark, the cows running
　　in the rain beside the fence, almost udder-
less, young and curious, their noses raised,
　　desperate to kiss me. Dream on. The rain
hissed like steak or fish in a skillet as I
　　leaned on an iron gate gritty with rust and
got my shoes snagged on a loop of barbed
　　wire and saw where hooves printed the black
earth with deep, impermanent hieroglyphs
　　that filled with reflections, rain silvering them
like mirror backs. Garlic mustard in flower –
　　tiny white starbursts – rank nettles, sorrel
waist high. I was thinking about my father
　　and the days he'd stood somewhere like this,
waiting for work or a bus in Crumpsall or
　　for rain to stop smoking over the roofs, the
city really burning one time in the Blitz,
　　though that was night. Thinking about my
sons who might one day think about me
　　in this scent of damp foliage and fleece,
the face of my watch steaming over and
　　needing a piss (rain does that; some water-
sympathetic thing), this poem at the back
　　of my mind let loose in a book, the cows
long gone to slaughter after lives of
　　ruminating pasture to cream. It struck
me as no small thing to see that crazed
　　elbow in the glass of time and it occurred
to me as utterly ordinary, the way all
　　miracles are mundane: rain whispering

itself to a kind of nothingness, streams
  gargling in spate, droplets shining on every
spear of grass, mist huffing from meadows
  of trodden thistle, disappearing from day's
mythic skin, the old terroir of dreams,
  the mind's forgetfulness it had drifted in.

Easter Sunday, Table Mountain

Under Devil's Peak
    burnt rocks fractured
        and falling.

A fiscal bird singing
    from the *fynbos*; that
        tanker far

out in ecumenical seas,
    a faded blue scattering
        serifs of foam.

The broiling city
    below: its quiet churches
        still mosques

its township choirs
    raising iron roofs.
        Erratic rains

spotting the dust;
    red-winged starlings,
        finches scattering

a kestrel rising
    with outspread wings
        hovering into an ocean

breeze, holding
    all this steady, flying
        at the same speed

as wind
    as waves
        as light.

Pilgrims

We found their nests, the dossing, hare-eyed
     men with beards: flattened grass, newspapers,
paper bags, sawn-open cans, whiskey bottles
     smelling of Christmas where a black and a white
terrier faced out; a circle of ash, a circle of
     scorched stone. We saw them on the road,
coats bunched with string, still trudging from
     Tobruk, Singapore, the Yalu river; retreating
through the sixties where we were children
     and they were their own footsore history on
the move, sometimes knocking at our back
     door to ask the missus for water or odd jobs,
selling something whittled from wood or
     twisted from wire, their teeth brown, their
fingernails dirt-blue, their smell the yeasty
     sawdust our hamster foraged in. Other times
we watched them follow the railway lines like
     rumours, boots knocking on tarred sleepers,
silhouetted against a parched sky, guncotton
     clouds, thoughts skittering on shining steel,
a haversack slung, eyes flinching towards
     us where we spied from stands of willow
herb. We found their messages – bent
     hazel twigs in hedgerows – thought they
fished the canal for pike or snared rabbits
     to live, scoring crusts from cafés, black tea
in a twist of paper, shillings from men who'd
     served, grizzling out hymns in the street, a
cloth cap held out. We envied them their
     campfires, jack knives, the world's easy gifts;
the way our fathers seemed to know them
     or know something never said, and softened,
offering their hands with words made so low
     their syllables could cushion the resting place
those pilgrims headed to: night calls mewling,
     a fevered moon, eye whites flaring, smoking
buckshee tabs to ash, minds gnawing at the
     rind of days; us watching for them, our faces
pressed to pale reflections in dark glass.

Abed

When that oak bed arrived
    I knew I'd die in it: lugging
it with a stranger, first
    footing dumb snow, his van
blinking at the road end, then
    timbers shouldered to our
upstairs room, a Calvary
    of stairs, a gloam of dawn.

I was a carpenter's child:
    shavings and pine tar my
playthings, the burr of the
    saw its own language where
I fed ringlets to the coke
    stove and a starling my father
nursed lay wimpled in lint.
    A wood-chiseller's child

I say, touching my chest
    where surgeons put my heart
back – a golden fish gasping
    in its raiment of blood – then
touching oak posts, slats, ribs
    of oak ringed by sullen waters
where seasons widened then
    sank. You're asking me about

the starling as if its dying there
    so many winters distant isn't
through; dust specks tumbling
    as you lay fresh sheets, flecked
oak under my fingers, grain
    furled hymnal-tight, the birds
in dark suits, in their hundreds,
    clearing their throats.

Earthworm

You're heading
    somewhere blindly,
all mucus and
    muscle, setae and gut,
true grit; a pulsation
    of soil, an inner-tube
of blood and shit
    racing for that damp
patch near the wall:
    the dark, the drain,
the sump of history,
    of fate, and nothing
near to hate except
    those thrushes singing
from the gate that
    they'll exterminate,
extirpate your kind
    for fun; poor little
mucoid fascist – no
    belt, no fist, no gun –
no wonder you're a
    little pink, in haste,
a real fink, on the
    run, hating the light,
loving the dark –
    yourself – the furtive
tunnel of the night.

Winston

I'm off to feed the village pig, my pockets
    full of freckled pears. Winston's snuffling

the yard, back turned, arse bare, busy with
    affairs of state, his snout in the trough, legs

mired in socks of mud. I call him and he
    comes apace: two hundred pounds of

lard, bacon, pudding blood. He's happy
    to see me, grunts as if he knows my

face – or I'm so deeply sad I imagine that.
    These small gifts make him happy though

the iron gate clangs shut: fruits gone
    bad from our bowl, a tickled gut when

he goes belly up to play: he's not like
    a pig in shit, he is one, foraging the yard

all day, thinking whatever pigs think
    in the bounty of their world. The pears

are gone, hurled to his humongous
    jaws. I think how quick he'd gorge

on me: Francesco Raccosta fed half
    dead to Calabrian swine: *Not a fucking*

thing left, his Mafioso rival, Simone
    Pepe opined post-prandially, *Not a*

hope. Unreal! admiring Frank's capacity
    to squeal like a pig while being eaten

by them: a fittingly post-modern
    trope for a criminally unwilling meal.

Winston's above paranoid alarm, doesn't
    seem to see his death beneath my charms:

the captive bolt, the gun's held breath,
    dark in its Teflon sheath. He's politely

chuffed by the treats we bring, batting
    his eyelashes, teetering on cloven toes,

chest puffed out just so: a pampered
    baritone about to sing; a die–hard–right

politico; *sus domesticus* unflitched;
    salt–shy pork; a plutocrat fattening.

Alpujarra

Sun is feathering snow on the high *sierras*, brazing
    blackness into backlit citrus gold. Wind farms hum

slowly, phantoms of a sea wind that follows the
    new highway north. The room is dark still, shutters

tied back, nets softly breathing. Across baked clay
    roofs cockerels call in this cool dawn that will birth

a shivering, airy heat: shaved ice shaken to a liquor
    of night-clarifying flames. The cockerels' throats shudder

in their bronze raiment, bristle in scalding blood:
    fuck you! fuck you! fuck you! Hard guys strutting in hay-

strewn yards; riling stallions under fig trees where
    fruit hangs dusky-green, raising a line of smoke in the

valley, a scent of scorched olive wood; rousing
    granjeros who rise to pour diesel, crank engines, turn

soil to a parched furrow their fathers muleploughed;
    waking the village women, their faces

blurred by sleep, jolting children, stirring time-
    strapped lovers who can't be found. What was sin

is ordinary now, our sleeping together: hair
    tangled, shoulders sun-burned, dreams ebbing

from pillows the way a tide leaves drenched
    sand glittering or night shades turn on heels of light.

Amatrice

The sound of dust sifting to dust; an almost
silence, almost touchable. We took

the new track built from rubble – the old hair-
pin road collapsing into woods –

through a mist of talc where they were pulling
down a house; past police cars, aid

trucks, houses cracked open in spoiled clutches
and hens running wild under our

tyres, over the whisper of fallen chestnut leaves.
The mountains were the same, we

guessed: clouds puffing out their slow, white
smoke above a village of tents, a

new school timbered by joiners from the north.
The main street tilted in my lens, the

church steeple that killed a family in their beds,
the old school fallen from itself into a

kind of ignorance. Workers who'd pulled the dead
from sleep joined our photograph:

volunteers, their eyes hard to bear. They took
our hands, didn't want to let us leave

just then, as if we were a lost future's children
straying home. *Amatrice*, they said,

bearing witness, their blue jackets torn at the
sleeves. *Amatrice*: its leaves shivering,

their palms unreadable, lying still in ours.

Steeplejacks

Clouds blow south behind
    the church's long, judgmental
spire – that finger of God.
    The way they move higher
and higher beyond the
    window makes things spin.
My head's just keeping
    track of that low jazz down-
stairs playing in a room
    where news lies unread
near a vase of wilting
    broom. I hear you close the
fridge. Now you're chopping
    rocket or thyme, now I see
a ladder fixed to the spire, its
    metal gleam. Two steeple-
jacks with nine lives each
    beetle up in yellow jackets
making a break for heaven
    without the awkward ritual
of prayer, just their caught
    breath, wind tugging, hearts
hammering, boots singing
    higher on the rungs. The track
changes, a flute lisps, a
    saxophone curls from a dead
man's lungs. Then a man shouts
    from the weather-vane, straddling
green wire that lightning climbs;
    his foot rings, steps higher then
steps again, then rings, until
    the last pane of blue is closed
by white and he blazes darkly
    and we pause – both of us – hearing
the immense height of things.

Black Shiver Moss

Boxing Day: its aftermath of cloud, its cheese-
    cloth of mist where Ingleborough's thorn trees

tremble in hoarse flurries, splitting glazed rocks. Shake-
    holes mutter dropped syllables under ribs of stone: ice-

raked, ice-cracked, gaunt against mud and rushes,
    the sour chiding of weather. A slowly rotting depth

of peat sucks rain from Black Shiver Moss, Black
    Shiver Ridge, Black Shiver – the thing itself – stark

soul-stealing sensation incarnate. God's Bridge is
    a speck in the valley's glaucous eye; now ruined

sheepfolds clatter from our hands; a multitude of
    sheep follow, treading gnawed beets, treading

gravity, rumps red from the tup. We had such
    faith in our bodies: now my white hair fumes

prophetic smoke. The viaduct's held by braced
    stone shrouds – another kind of faith – that

mason's raft ventured on a quaking bog, its
    caterpillar gait a parable of patient, man-killing

labour. North of us twin rainbows curve into
    space, speared by geese, falling to a river's rain-

smeared mirrors where lowing water-bound
    beasts trudge at land's dissolution. We stare

at what hangs there: the word and its world
    and the sky of the world, split into radiance.

Fire Management

They were burning off the *fynbos*, managing a fire
    that couldn't jump the road, though wind drove it

towards the shark-tooth mountains of the Cape.
    There was smoke, of course, mist occluding the faded

sky, white cuticles of sand below us where the oceans
    came in – Atlantic and Indian – seething together around

the last needle of rock where it pointed south to
    the Pole and a stumpy lighthouse rose from steps and

a signpost mocked us with destinations that spelt
    home: London, New York, Sydney, Rome. Baboon

droppings on the path, so you clung to my arm, wild
    at the thought of them; a guy in winkle pickers went past

teetering on a sloping stone with a camera as his family
    watched. *One slip*, we said, but they just laughed, Francophone

Africans from somewhere far northwest of there. Later
    at the Cape of Good Hope, we found the beach and a colony

of cormorants hunched at the rocks, crowding out gulls
    and terns, the waves coming slant, your hair blowing, your

eyes bright with salt, half closing them at its sting.
    We drove back into flames and smoke, the fire tenders

waving us through as if the whole of Africa was burning.
    Tonight, your eyes said, flaring against black rock fuming

with light, *our last*. Tomorrow, the plane lifting you to
    an English spring, the continent all ash beneath its wings.

Elterwater

The lake was silver leaf ruffled by sun;
there were still some squalls of rain,
hurried as if missing the show; families
scurrying for their cars, waterproofed,
heads low, the beer garden packed with
bikes and knackered blokes. Further back
the hills seemed to dissolve, rain quarrying
them and throwing the spoil to heaven.
Half-soaked we trekked the lake from
memory and that was unreliable to say
the least and we were walking it back-
wards so things looked different though
they were probably the same – thirty
years hardly scuffs the Langdale moss.
There were dappled cows at the southern
tip, stretching to reach low boughs,
Herdwick sheep grazing the fells with
floppy looking necks and legs; a shepherd
with her dogs and crook, bent with age.
We'd lost the lake now, climbing the path
to Colwith, then Fletcher's Wood where
we saw a sparrow hawk who just glared
at us from a fir tree, she was so pumped
with rage or hate. The path ran with water
where we unlatched the gate to join the
road; then the lake again, just a little
tarnished; then our room in a pub I
misremembered, its sharp, hot shower
before we ate. The bed was hard and
high and we slept late, so when we
woke it was already nine. I reminded
you we'd driven here in our Morris Minor
once, made love in woods dusky with
bluebells and you laughed at that, of all
things, hooking my arm, saying we'd
miss breakfast, our own funerals.

Les Couleurs

They line up where the cabbie's curt nod
    placed them as we came – *les couleurs* –
insinuated by his sleight of speech, waking
    on wasteland under palm trees and
bougainvillea, beside the flensed whalebone
    of Our Lady's church. They clutch paper cups,
glimpse early morning wraiths of work,
    stashing sleeping gear, waking the teenage
girl who joined them and they kept safe.
    Now the heating spice of piss, stale baguette,
sour wine: a new day, the empire's spittle
    drying on their backs, yachts bisecting the
bay in blue quadrants, sky shivering
    the scorch of water to liminal grey.
Pale-skinned girls stroll to the beach,
    too sensible to stray from the *Promenade
des Anglais*; those already tanned, toss
    highlights in their hair, make for the sickle
of sand to turn their slowly basting wave.
    Streets glare, etched with shadows, their
heat reminding us how bodies fail, fold
    into future tides, into cities that reflect them-
selves, insatiably alive, self-scrutinised
    through glass. The priest at the soup kitchen
tends to children of a failed god: they
    watch us bring our bags from the hotel;
their eyes are almonds, pistachios, nubs
    of honey, olives glinting green/brown;
figs pulp underfoot where pigeons strut
    beneath the brass medallion of the sun.

Argon

When you're not here there's rain
    sifting onto slates, the porch light's
bleb of molten resin spun around its
    filament; midges dying with lit wings,
house martins leaving for the shimmy
    of Saharan air; a novel laid under a table
lamp – all fiction and our lives conflated
    there – and rain falling, its fabulations
filling each dimension, expanding a lost
    summer's legendary wetness: the river
simmering, net furled on the tennis
    court where I watched a white owl
blunder into trees to break its vow
    of loneliness. Even before this, there
was some urgent thing you said
    I didn't hear, lugging your bags to the
car, half-turning when you turned
    to leave, pouting like a starlet, fluffing
first gear. I swept you away like dust
    from my sleeve, impatient with every
thing that might lay waste to precious
    thoughts alone; now long days dusk to
ghostly nights, wraiths of future life.
    You're gone as if our sleepy pupal
past has died, dissolving to hatch
    me: goldwing imaginal circling argon
in hot glass, spirals of tungsten, atoms
    that endlessly collide.

Stella Rossa

*'The April sun will continue to rise and shine its brilliance
from the blue sky and the light, pure air over woods and green pastures.'*
— Bruno Luppi

An orange moon sags on forest hills;
    streams unchoke, foaming after that
last drench of rain, their other language
    clamouring. Swallows dive into the

vortex of migration, finding thermals,
    rising on wing-flickers that blur place,
movement, moment. Back home they'll
    be chittering on wires, starched shirt-

fronts carrying the same wine stain
    over Yorkshire. Here, a column of
cloud pinks up before the sun's last
    exhortations, your fingers' pressure

on my arm, your eyes lit April-green.
    Earlier we walked through hay fields,
past a gutted church: its cracked tiles,
    smashed stucco, plaster dust, its walls

scrawled by graffiti and smoke. We
    toiled to that village on the hill through
wild pea blossom, strewn barley
    straw, an overhang of hazels where

pigeons quarrelled and rose and settled
    underfoot, the draught of their wings
cooling us. We rested at the village pump,
    shirts stiff with sweat, puzzling out

remembrance etched in granite. An
    old woman passed us with cardboard
to recycle — as if this was ordinary, as
    if this was everyday. She asked us

Where from? and our English/Italian
　　　set her weeping at the written stone,
her father and sisters brought white-
　　　faced to the September sun to die

for all *Il Lupo* did, reprisals spilled in
　　　the stars of their blood. Now we're
watching from another village, hiding
　　　in plain view, our fugitive selves lost

in alleyways that riddle each hill.
　　　Wells are mossed with damp where
water's moon glints deep, bullfrogs
　　　pipe a forlorn lust and there'll be

fireflies in the meadows where we
　　　walked, that woman's grief haunting
a clean-swept square. *Why kill when
　　　we have to die?* you ask and I can't

reply, that pillar of cloud stained
　　　by the fallen sun. Then church bells –
each a moment out of time – pealing
　　　down the valley, one by one.

★ 'Stella Rossa' was the name given to the partisan resistance to the
WWII Nazi occupation of Italy. 'Il Lupo' was the *nom de guerre* of
their leader, Mario Musolesi. The epigraph is from a poem by the
partisan Bruno Luppi, translated by Lisa Samson from the memorial
at Castel Vittorio, Liguria.

Froglet

A diamond-tip shard
      of flint, a jade arrowhead
flirted under the saffron
      trumpets of courgette
flowers just beyond my
      brogue's print on dark
rotted soil; hatched
      from the ragged spawn
a cold spring let into
      our pond; now amphibious,
lunged, miniature;
      perfect the way small
things are. I thought
      I'd catch it for you, open
my fist – my scrolled-
      hand like parchment,
like my father's now –
      show it you to marvel
at. Not a hope: it's gone
      again, a tiny flickering
miracle, a gleam of eye-
      shine, a dwarf god growing
into lordship of its world,
      peering at thunder clouds,
darkly immanent, blinking
      away raindrops that slide
from leaf hairs, angelica-
      green zucchini stems,
magnifying everything.

Veldtschoen

for John Colton

Darker by a thousand leagues than when
    I hefted them in Cleary's shop that day,

smelling of leather newly tanned: now
    dubbin, sheep shit, river clay. Eyelets

worn to brass, noses scarred as twin
    pit bulls, liners grafted at each inner

heel, zugged leather brown as chestnut
    hulls. Soled a dozen times, stripped, re-

sewn, nailed close as Veldtschoen moulded
    on my ghost, bought where your dad got

his before a self-hitched rope swung
    Cleary from a roofing post. Now whoever

leaves last gets both pairs: our deal to
    celebrate the way we trekked up fells by

night, before a bypass left me welted
    with thoracic scars. That riven corset's

laced shoe-tight, a new lease on the old
    life; not dead yet, though my ribs creak when

dreams are rife. *Good for a few more miles,*
    young Cleary said, wrapping them in the spectre

      of his father's smile.

Rain at Franschoek

A soft day washes heat from mountains, the
pass curving through rock where baboons
watch their young dangling one-handed from

conifer fronds. Rain is slaking orchards,
those yellowed vines. Not African rain – rain
that fluxes landslides, thrums in your head,

beating away blood, raising a heat-drenched
thunder, torrenting ochre dust – but a sly
rain that could be English, dampening spinach

leaves, loosening whitethorn blossom, earth's
garlic stink of spring. It's sudden against
the windows at 4:00am, then gone, its faint

susurration a prayer to the monkey gods of
drought. Rain was sent to clean peaks where
clouds were brewing yesterday and I was

slithering down through prickly pears, honey
bush, loose stone, feeling breath tear in my chest,
watching poplars turn above Dutch gables, a

reservoir flex. Tomorrow it will rain again –
the way days turn, the way a drum makes and
keeps time, its syncopated snare/bass beat.

The hands of my watch are luminous; cool air
saunters in with a pied crow's mockery of
dawn, my pulse bumping, its tributaries choked,

its lightning strike three days hence, when
everything will be electric, everything white
in my afterglow; dry leaves crumbling from

my hands, those baby primates tumbling from
tree tips, the mountains shattered by light.
And everything clear, just for a moment,

everything liquefied into a sweet immensity:
autumn dust, oblivion, clouds pronouncing
themselves, rain darkening the road.

* Franschhoek is in the Cape region of South Africa. Settled by
  Huegenot refugees from France in 1688, its poplars, vineyards and
  Dutch style farmhouses give it a European aspect, though its backdrop
  is one of ancient and dramatic mountain ranges.

Janáček Sonata

1.X.1905

'*The white marble of the steps of the Besední dům in Brno. The ordinary labourer František Pavlík falls, stained with blood. He came merely to champion higher learning and has been slain by cruel murderers.*'
　　　　　　　　　　　　　　　　　　　　　　　－ Leoš Janáček

We breathe the clarities of haunted
　　　air: it carries all frequencies, brings

Janáček's sonata for a dead carpenter,
　　　František Pavlík, bayoneted a century

ago in Brno, for his love of learning.
　　　Now here with you an apocalypse later

faintly hungover after a night with
　　　friends, his *klavierwerke* chiming through

our rooms where this late January
　　　afternoon turns *pianissimo* towards

night, shading into *foreboding* and
　　　death, as his movements have it.

But this morning I saw young cattle
　　　gathered at a manger, their breath's

memory frozen, their brute hides
　　　stark with mud and beautiful. So

I hold it optimistic and dear, this
　　　moment: minims of winter sun

strewn upon our bed; Pavlíc's young
  life lost; the elegy that seemed so frail

when pitched against main force, cast
  to the Vitava to float away. *Its pages*

like white swans, Janáček said, gazing
  from the parapet at his own fury and

despair silenced there – though
  they returned to him before he

died, those evanescent wings
  scuffing the future's unstilled air.

★ Janáček composed this work for piano in 1905 after the death
of František Pavlík at a demonstration for a Czech university in
Brno. Dissatisfied, he destroyed the manuscript, throwing it into the
Vitava river, but a copy survived and was performed for him when
aged seventy.

Fado

I love the sound of Fado:
the way melisma makes old-style
calligraphies of air; then those fleet
guitars, their twinned octaves sounding
plangent steps over a frail bridge
where we imagine beautiful
incestuous orphans bathe
in fallen peonies.

To attend to Fado is to drink
the darkest, most resolute of wines,
vinho tinto more turgid than blood –
think instead the clotted, inexpressibly
dense hearts of stars pressed from
clearest, most abandoned tears,
think shadows of all a city's
shuttered bars.

Steps pass to the window's
billowing gauze, patter in streets
where lovers' farewells linger as
rancorous applause, where wounded
duellists moan, earthquakes rive
imperial destinies and Fate's
dread tumbrils clatter over
ruined cobblestones.

I love the forthright, drunken
songs of Fado, its slurred patois
of nightingales and Portuguese, its
hopeless pleas wrung from deepest
cobalt blue, *intaglio* of the stone-
washed shirts of fishermen, the
clouded eyes of women
gazing to azure seas.

If we should part before
life ends, let Fado lament love's
death: its haste to consummate the
unremitted joy that we once
lived, its eternal brevities of
touch, its teeth clenched
in ecstasy, its cruel but
vital waste of breath.

Girl at Cam Fell

It was a Sunday, which meant nothing;
I was walking eastwards into a moon's
unworldly hallucination, into that stillness
inside me; the path's braided stone scarf
blown against the fell, unfurling ridge by
ridge. Sky burned white by cold, sun brazing
the horizons, my shadow's broken spear
against the track; rock scarred where a
trailer touched down or a Landrover
jolted its load of ewes, the collie eager
to harry its flock, the flock scattered in
rushes that burned as bronze sheaves or
pale-blue stooks. Just enough heat to
raise creosote scent from gates, frost's
white nape hair on their shadow-side.
I turned to face sun's miasma, land's
sunken western edge, the bay sweltering
in scattered rays, the bridleway sweating
rills from shattered ice, when you appeared –
head down with that bouncing walk, so
young and alone and afraid as I spoke.
We passed, then turned to glimpse each
other: I gauged the larch plantation's
selvedge where it halved a hill, you lifted
your foot to the wall, tucking in a lace –
somehow here from nowhere I could guess –
air stirring what had passed as solitude, colder
now, fraying between us like a seam.

Little Egret

Sky is streaked gold, apricot,
　　purple; its broken contrails die as
photons dunked in sunset's haze.

　　The meadow is flooded, tinned with
light's copper/nickel flux where coot
　　and mallard feed, a cock pheasant's

brazen throat strikes broken
　　chords, a white water bird alights to
settle its downfolded wings –

　　a pilgrim robed at water's shrine
a phosphor-bright albino blown
　　astray to its indifferent northern kin.

Water bellows through drenched
　　fields, flinging sea trout as sticks: now
this spirit restless as lambent

　　flame lights the solstice, the
shortest day then longest
　　night rehearsing longer absence.

I look south and it vanishes,
　　flown away to grace or drawn
down through earth's mantle

　　to its molten core. When you
left I knew that you'd come
　　back this way, a migrant bird

straying to my life, resting
　　your wings where I could find
you, lost before the dark.

La Maison Bleue

Before I died, we rented a blue house
on a narrow street that twisted down
to a river bridge's leaping arch.

The house had photographs of a family
just like mine: the parents happy back
in time, looking sideways to the future,

their children born into a Technicolor
age that left them fading from walls: all
handmade brick, lime render and stone

the tincture of honey or that quaint
gesture – a curl of hair in a silver locket.
Since the house was finished in oak, I

thought of my coffin in a black car, my
grown-up children by the graveside, a
baby I'd never know in someone's arms.

At night we left a casement open and
a bat flew in, its echolocation bouncing
from the angles of the room: I could

see it as a cat's cradle (that old
marmalade Tom chancing the dusk)
or a parable with many meanings.

When I woke it was under a heavy quilt:
a smell of mice, the sharp sounds of
birds in our fig trees, the river tugging

its fish to face the current, ants at
their labour, a lizard growing a new
tail. There was a market in the

square, a bodhrán's solemn pulse
making it Sunday. When I reached
for a glass of water my fingerprints

were magnified and white and very
bright. There was a dark stain on
the coverlet, the vine outside glowing

green as if sap was flame. You were
saying something about the heat –
still sleepy, still beautiful – shuffling

into a summer skirt of dark blue
plums; my shoes on the floor, their
footprints heading somewhere.

Brambles

These woods are rife with bluebell scent each
        spring: now we're up to our hips in bracken and
itchy autumn heat, pulling at fruit glossy as paint,

sloes blue in the hedgerows, yellow sycamore
        stars, nettles, tormentil, mushrooms hoofed
over into tractor ruts. The more we pick the

more we need: some old urge to gather and
        feed making us peer under leaves, reach into
stinging shadows that hawthorns and oaks

harbour. I say it's pure sex, pulling instinct to
        the past, but you're laughing, swinging a gravid
carrier bag at the gate where Limousins thud

the field and a pair of buzzards circle and
        mew and a blizzard of rooks falls into trees.
You're thinking of jam, the freezer, black-

berries at Christmas when the boys are home
        and the stoves lit, wet snow blowing from the yard
to the log pile, the vegetable beds, the pond's

cataleptic stare. Our hands are gangland
        killer's mitts as we sidle through fern and cow
parsley – a single fly agaric bitten on the verge,

pheasants breaking cover, a cockerel calling at
        the farm below the ridge, the toll of wet clay
on our boots, sun westering, a carmine sky

        warning us with all its dizzy weight.

Midland Rail

Crows over stubble, like a Dutch painting;
a bandage of mist, everything wounded –

the red clay, seeping sky, burnt trees
charred by dream-flamed hours of night.

It's been a year since she went home to
patch its remnant of childish time. Her

book's forgotten now instead of this: a
freight train's rapid admonition on rails

smeared with dawn, cattle stooped at
the treeline, anointed by hefted sun.

A trinity of cooling towers coughs out
clouds; birch leaves blaze yellow slag;

flat rivers carry away light. Her face at
the window, pressed between glass; her

eye-pits brimming over a white house,
grazing horses, the canal's printout.

Wheels sing it: *you were never here, never
here, never here* where blind factories

fall, bulrushes spike the mill lodge and
an old man casts a line, waist deep in

reflections. Two herons stagger – stage
drunks faltering on scooped wings:

she sees them lifting mythically-scented
feet, flying to locations their shadows

announce, like the next town and the
next. Around her they pull down bags,

check cellphones, search platforms for
those they have loved or may have

loved or love still; now doors open,
recursive, repeating dawn's chill.

Spectre

Sometimes, waking early,
    you try to remember your
future life and it's faint as

    voices playing through a half-
tuned radio or wine that's
    past its best – present and

absent at the same time.
    You think things must always
be renewed yet they are some-

    how just themselves and less
than something lost that
    mattered then. Today mist

is douching fields where
    May blossom has startled us
close to wonderment –

    every tree its own spectre,
hiding its untouchable, un-
    knowable self. And through

all that, the past you kept
    once, crying to come in, to
re-enter a space it knows,

    has marked with an old erotic
scent, unfaithfully rubbing its
    neck at the window, always

hungry its ears *en pointe*, its
    pupils split green stones, its
yawn fanged with boredom.

Rough Fell

In December, Cumbrian debatable lands yield
more stone than grass, so each year they winter

with us, white-fleeced refugees trailered here,
noses full of these fields' southern sweetness.

Today, they all point the same way as if this
earthly paradise magnetised them, solemn-faced,

meditative and still, ignoring me, attending to
the plainchant of wind in our valley, its chill

skimmed from the Irish Sea. Each year we greet
them, glad they're here, but what stirs them to

stumble into gangs or turn from us or approach
as mendicants, I can't say. Their unspun coats

gleam in gossamer dreads: rough fell sheep
stepping through thistles, tongues rasping at

grass, ruminative, serene beyond all worldly
harm. I'm full of my own unworthiness facing

such scholastic calm: they muse on, hefted by
an ovidian god – surefooted, confident, elect.

But as I turn to face that drowned divinity of
sun, I'd swear their knock knees genuflect

in wonder at the night, its sleight of dark,
its ungrazed leys where stars flock.

Bisoprolol Fumarate

They tamed my pulse with small
white pills; now blood flicks steady
as a whip, the way all time seems
to exist, blipping at my wrist
behind a scar the cannula etched:
the present moment slipping into
shade, the future moment brightly
fetched, its sea-change unfathomably
strange. I climb this long, green hill
to life; hands trudge captive on a
chronographic dial, measure my pulse
against earth's pull: that faint *ka-boom*
of hatches clanging on a sunken hull,
doors closing in a darkening room.

Bypass

White hanks wad the valley's throat, farms
    and trees float, a buzzard fights off a crow;

cattle run beside the road, hooves churning
    mud; calves follow, villages sleep, sun mithers

a bolster of cloud where evaporating dreams
    are heaped. I slip past the shut pub, drop gears

to take a twisting hill, fingers frozen to the
    bars, chain slithering on the hub, lungs glad

of breath's chill blade. A rider appears, then
    is lost in mist, another light-anointed shade;

a pheasant tumbles to the facts of flight, rooks
    hunch on sagging wires, my shadow's balanced

on the squeal of tyres. I catch my double at the
    junction, coming silently behind: he turns across

me, blind, not knowing that I'm here, yet we're
    two of a kind, him heading west as I face dawn.

Three pale palomino foals are stunned by sun;
    thistles defrost in streams of down and spider

silk, a tractor turns with its spiked bale, the day
    raw with diesel and dung from the milking sheds.

You're waking now in our quiet house to a
    hot shower, rough towels, Colombian coffee

and Cumbrian bread, honey from bees that
    doze in the covenant of their hive. I'm cycling

home to show you that I'm still alive:
    a breathless revenant, not six years dead.

Last Day in Obs

Driving towards Table Mountain for the
  last time: sheer slopes, clouds buffering,
Lion's Head dunked in mist, only Signal

Hill clear with its eyelash of trees. A trash
  of white birds goes over and I don't know
them, can't name them, wonder why I've

spent so much of life out of my depth.
  Townships go past – ribbed iron roofs,
red oxide, scrambled planking and smoke –

a woman pushing a trolley down the road
  as if it's an aisle at the Pick n' Pay, a mechanic
welding a bakkie's blown exhaust on

wasteland, no mask, his eyes cratering;
  a horse and cart, like the rag–bone man I
knew as a kid, cauterizing our back alley

with his yell, the horse trotting, the reinsman
  staring south where sun stumbles and another
ridge of mountains starts to burn. I'm heading

for Obs, twin of the scuzzy brick-built town
  where I was raised, but gone New Age: all body-
pierced *baristas* and tattoo joints, its old-style

drunks begging for grog at wheelie bins, out-
  side supermarkets, on piss–darkened pavements
in stinking urban African heat. Now a lane

closure. Fuck! A guy in high viz genuflecting,
      waving his red flag at a line of cars or me; the
view vaporising to laundry steam then falling

as rain that wipers smear but can't take away
      though they try and try as if this is a new kind
of purgatory. Now a cone of sun widens,

glares, smoulders, and the mountain is
      there again: a crumbling deity, a mask of
imperturbable wisdom, calm, or hate; a

fluke of time exfoliating as I brake, slip
      onto this freeway slick with bloodshot
lights that lead me somehow home.

* 'Obs' is the shortened form of 'Observatory', a district of Cape Town
  that adjoins Woodstock. Many industrial premises there have now been
  gentrified or been taken over by New Age entrepreneurs and artisans.

Dogs

There are these dogs, trained to bark and yelp at
epilepsy's synesthetic blip; hounds that got so

far forward of their game they could know a tonic
clonic seizure's coming on and whine and scratch

and run for help until their owners battened hatches
in anticipation of the storm their brains let rip.

I wonder if those same dogs, cocking a super-sensile
ear, could feel the aura of a poem coming near:

a sonnet's low vibration, its tessellated rhyme, its
voltaic shock a cool-tiled floor stepping to an

opened door; a brief lyric gliding down glass, clear
as rain; haiku rippling a lake's green pane with

spots of fleeting immanence; the maze of a sestina,
echolalia of a villanelle in which lines persist as

repetitious sound, as lost and found, so writing is
a practised innocence. Afterwards, when the

poet is sleeping soundly and the poem is resting
on the page, the dogs slobber water in a bowl

or softly howl to slake their inner, immolating rage,
shaking stray couplets from their coats, smelling

indelibly of verse that made words sing, their fading
faint as ether at a landing strip, a ghost vaporizing.

Spotted Woodpeckers

From the Bramley to the rowan
    to the black cherry to the svelte air
over the valley, its pelt of dew

slung upon stone shoulders.
    The sparrow hawk goes over or a
cuckoo – we guess at silhouettes –

their hardy throwing back of
    atmosphere and early morning
shade. Now these light-spun

pendants glitter in the apple
    tree – jet, ivory, ruby – sleekly
hatchet its seething bark.

They hunt for grubs when
    stalking the hot, cloacal sex
that birds have, their feathers

trembling with mites. Tonight
    little owls will smooth dark's
mass into the valley with

calls that bring stillness as
    their aftershock. Then brightest
planets swing close, radio-

active pearls on a swart
    breast: Jupiter and Venus, their
counterpoint before dawn

when the mind is a temple
    of self-worshipping doubt –
thought's poison sheaf laid

bare as mistletoe in a sepulchre.
    We'll know them if morning comes
and they return, breast to

breast, their jewelled bodies
    lapped by flames, their longing
wings, their hollow bones.

A Rising

Up at six to bake the dough that swelled with wild
spores all night, its sour dream leavening the dark.

Low sun comes with early day, cattle epic under
thorn blossom, meadow grass glassy with dew.

Shadows stretch from the roots of trees, fish ghosts
steer the gill, finning stone. Light seeps through

glass, a child snores upstairs, a toilet flushes, then
the blurred tread of footsteps. She's knocking hot

bread from the tins: its burnt rye smell, its glaze of
milk that was grass bent under rain, a Holstein's

tongue. In March, before he passed, three blackbirds
quarrelled here, cocksure duellists in tight frock

coats: now they pour this quintessence from their
throats, the purified loss of song. She sits with

a book of poems tracing the crewel-work of another
mind, its fey twist and chance. Images transpire through

space more real than this lit room, its cooling loaves.
She wonders who will come to share them first: her

boys, still sleeping with their wives? Her grandson,
his cheeks a flush of pillow-heat and apple bloom?

Cattle raise their heads, stark and huge, staring at the
house where she is spellbound in stanzas, the hush

of rooms. Words fall out of order, rise again to make
meaning, the pages turning, faint as indrawn breath.

Snow Burst

Driving home, wipers
    blinking away snow, the
        road whitening, air parting

in scattering meteor
    showers startled from our
        inner-eye: shucked galaxies

whirling in our headlamp
    beams, tumbling light and
        time, collapsing us into the

selves who set off days ago:
    springing the Yale, switching
        off household appliances

stacking the car boot
    with bags and a feather
        quilt, starting the engine

burning a deliquescent
    forest pumped from ancient
        shales to navigate the road.

We follow this blaze of
    earthly light and heavenly light
        which is only snow, its delirious

whiteout a blaze of fractals
    we're so caught up in that
        we repeat ourselves, forget

its entropy will be some
    deep tarnish of the way
        ahead: a melting into night

that's soft, dark, ripe
    as sleep.

Pigeonnier

He walks through a cloud of blue moths –
    one for each apostle – into a round tower

with a peaked *chapeau* of tiles, the oak door
    rotted, wasps fierce in the vine, limestone

steps hollowed. Rows of nesting boxes dark
    as the eyes of city whores: pigeons sleeping,

a wedge of sun chiseling mica through dusky
    air. Now the quiet clamour of roosting birds

kept for the eggs he candles in the sacristy;
    for the sweet meat of their breasts and dung

dug into the Abbé's onion beds; for music of
    a sort: the crooning of forbidden sex, blood

bubbling from a man's cut throat. The boy
    reaches to their stink, peering at novices

working the pump below: their creamy thighs
    and sleek-dipped heads, their oxter hair and

sideways looks; soapy laughter, stiff nipples,
    wide eyes and slender hands. Now this back-

plumage black as smeared soot; iridescent
    necks, this underwing down dense with heat

and lice and suffocating dark. Their amber
    eyes stare incuriously as he kills, wringing

out last sobs of life, lining them up neat
    as martyrs cut down from a cross of air.

Last Star

All rivers run east: sky shatterings,
    ice-melt shadows, they shimmy under
pylons and cooling towers, between
    cabbage fields, beyond houses whose
grey windows stare in at themselves.
    This train flashes on and off and on
over flatlands as random code;
    kestrels are checkmated kings;
ponds drag silted light to tangled
    alder roots, duckweed, a meniscus
of polystyrene scum. Frogs bask in
    freezing mud, their amber eyes
hatching future lifeforms, blazing in
    deep strategic sleep. The Humber
Bridge pulls tight to the skyline –
    all vertiginous temptation; clouds
blue as scrawled Quink, rain at the
    windows, its sound of tiny suckers
pulling clear; bushes flitting by in
    black bison herds. That squaddie
sleeping could be dead at Crécy,
    the train rocking terraced streets,
their slow TV blues shuffling into
    dusk, their bared intimacies scrolling
by. Now that rep in a striped suit
    rising to coil his laptop lead like a
tie after a funeral. Now Leeds
    burning at the horizon, simmering
in its Bessemer of light – the last
    star in the universe sucked deep
into its own gravity, collapsing
    with massive life.

Cape Town Garden

Election Day, April, 2014

A turtle dove flutters to the cement
    fountain, sipping from a cherub's feet;
ibis shriek overhead, their cries rend
    timber, split skull bones, screech out

quarried stone to the steel guts
    of ships docked here a century ago.
Evening ripples on these ochre walls;
    a crooked tree leans over the sun, a

lavender patch. Power lines sag, iron
    roofs bloom with rust, the sky clears
of cirrus. Table Mountain is out of sight
    but crumbling still, sifting to Green

Point, Camps Bay, Cape Flats – that haze
    of dust and heat-wavering roads where
figures wait or walk behind their shadows:
    stick-people from this far distance, their

mouths dried by an ancient thirst, sucking
    a pebble so enduringly smooth that
history surely intended it. Footsoles strike
    the hard shoulder under sky scoured by

a westward slinking sun: shadows stride
    shrink, stride. So now it's upright bodies
we imagine, their level hands, their clouded
    eyes unblinking at faint horizons. The

dove is alert, listening, its wings brushing
    the rim, hushing every hue of grey: cloud-
wisps, summit-mist, sea-fret – all that lies
    beyond this garden in the Cape Town sun.

Now it tilts its bill to drink a cool illusion:
    water's mirage shimmering at the brim.

Saving Daylight

Our way of shunting off the
dark, this unkindly lie; winding
on the clocks to lengthen day

as dusk thickens a cobalt sky;
re-setting my watch, the cooker's
digital display. Later, when I

should be sleeping still, rising in
the night's small hours to finish
off a book in the chill of the

stove burned low. Wind in the
flue sucks sparks from ash,
brings the kindling thought of

you and what loss is and how
it persists just as the supple light
of day is stretched to make

finite things go far: paraffin,
candles or coal, a plough, the
war. More is less and less is

more: playing out extra time;
blood's seepage on the killing
floor. This assassinating dark

surprises us, available as if for
hire. Now it's comforting to draw
down blinds; the window's view

wound out of sight, these sable
folds pulled tight; the hands of
widows wringing out last light.

Diablo

Sky is a white crucible fired to ceramic blue.
    I turn to watch martins scour it, a herring
        gull balance on pantiles, mocking the sea

where it kneels over and over, a grey widow
    worshipping cold stones, waves scattering,
        small boats fitful at anchor, hard weather

to come. A church bell quarters the hours:
    nothing moves on the mountain – maybe a
        single car glinting, that's all – white villas

slumbering, rock drenched in early sun,
    los pinos scattering, those last planets fading
        apart. Salt stinging on shingle's tongue, that

low hiss of air on water like a language
    labouring to be heard or the silence in steep
        streets where tourists sleep late. The glint

of radio masts, their frequencies teeming
    in invisible shoals, a drover's road broken
        into dashes that stammer upwards between

white rock and wild vines, birds floating as
    motes in the day's milky eye. I've got my
        hands on the tiled balcony, my face to the

sun, heat on my temples making me squint
    into shadows, making me remember all this
        going on when I'm rendered back to dust,

sifting in a funeral plume, a devil twisting to
    escape into smoke, molecules, space. Pages
        of my life curling, their meaning blackening,

emptied of my own self; my body gaseous,
    my soul incandescent again, weightless and
        pure, my poems burning – patient as stars.

Aphasia

Genesis

Born to it: a city of smoke-dyed rivers,
    cotton towns packing our captive souls

into brick terraces, into mills bright as
    ocean-going liners where loom and frame

choirs chanted litanies of servitude,
    their chimneys a petrified forest drifted

with spores of cotton, asbestos, rayon.
    Our working kind saved for funerals, were

burned, scattered, buried nameless under
    green mounds. Urban, liminal, the moors

heaped a tweed horizon, sun glittering on
    farmhouse windows, cars crawling beyond

the town's long decay, its stink of latex as
    migrants worked the rubber mill, moving

striplit behind iron grilles when we stared in
    from the street: our first black men, labouring

at hot, intractable machines. Their shadows
    made them gods striving in the clash of patois:

Lancastrian-Jamaican, its soft syllabic rain
    sifting the machines' thunder of electric light.

Goldenrod and fireweed, buddleia and
    foxgloves, bluebells and cabbage whites

in all the gardens, and bees drunk on
    their own fervour of industry. All those

lives, journeys, tongues, all those words:
    a city, describing itself as endlessly elsewhere.

Exodus

Schooled, freed, leaving the city
        for that line of hills, for lime-white
scars, taking the road north. That
        bright-edged air was light

and light was future time, its
        flux, its superfluity. I felt I owned
those fells quartered in stone, or
        they owned me before I came

through history: such *déjà vu*, that
        mind-made familiarity. I woke to
shorn meadows, each with its
        own hay barn; flour-nosed sheep,

hills' canticles of rain spewing
        speech from flooded workings,
venting peat-rich vowels,
        guttural, ancestral, already

deep in my way of saying
        things.

Toponymy

Muker is Norse: Keld, Gunnerside,
        Thwaite, Swale, Grinton, Reeth –
all migrant-named, the tongue rolling
        in foreign grit.

Noon heat climbs as stratus in sky's
        china blue, spreading a mycelium
spawn. Turned headstones pave
        graveyards, face-down

on their holy texts, pressing dates
        that open and close centuries – wild
flowers in a stone book – recording
        each life's shrunken

sentience. Field gates sprung
        with steel where a nailed boot-sole
served once, slapping timber against
        hewn uprights that

thud, shudder, loosen. Clog irons
        struck out this way, wore grooves
in dirt paths before those synoptic
        gospels were laid:

lead miners trudging from unholy
        dreams to labour, pick and shovel
heads hushing each pent gill.
        That lode's all spent:

galena smelted, wrought to
    musket balls, rifle rounds, pipe-
work, pewter, solder, guttering,
    earthenware glaze and

church roofs. Now spoil-heaps
    that seized crusher left, wrecked
washways, rusted gears, smashed
    timber, trolleys, roofless

shacks, sodden stone-lined shafts
    boring into hills to drain moss
of rain that slants, smokes,
    fumes into a new century.

Leadwork

Cheap imports bled out the trade, prices
    falling fast as shucked slag. They left in flocks,

in droves: America, Australia, Canada, the
    New World mineral-rich to miners skilled

as fairytale dwarfs, taking out their gnarled
    Yorkshire speech then losing it. Trade wars,

then the real thing – Spion Kop, Mons,
    Paschaendale – emptying these valleys like

a churn. Leaving for steady rations, England's
    soiled glory and shilling, for the liberties of a

slipshod imagining. Crushed into troopships,
    the dale's clay, dust and mud under their fingernails

and, still to come, their toil in Picardy: pick
    and shovel work, walling with sandbags, sagging

corpses, sleeping in a drowned sap or shelled
    church, remembering the Swale's chill against

their hands where they took a girl to ford
    shallows after Sunday chapel's gleeless drone

to see her shriek and hop from rock to rock,
    her skirts pulled high above neat ankle bones.

Legacy

Fern and harts tongue rife,
    another season dead in the
fire hole, grass burying the
    flue where flame ran, where

smoke fumed to arsenic
    crystals. This furnace burned
lurid as a sacking against the
    dark of day and night, as if

the longboats were back.
    Whinberries, bracken, black-
mouthed shooting butts, fell-
    sides patched pale with turf

cuttings, the burned heather
    bleached, the peat store's Inca
ruin sunk. Here a bankrupt
    gentry disinherit labour's

legacy. Range Rovers bring
    them to pony treks, the shoot –
grouse coveys break with
    choked cries, the guns'

hammers cracking wild air,
    wind carrying their calls
away, the holy ghost of
    drizzle haunting daylight:

Surrender Moss, Healaugh Crag,
    Barras Top; North Rake, Hanging
Stone, Wetshaw; Old Gang Beck,
    Flincher Gill, Reeth High Moor.

Reliquary

The railway station's iron
    lines lead nowhere now:
a museum, its reliquary of

pails and butter churns,
    its nostalgia nagging us
with caried teeth. Rust

pitting rails, cast wheels
    fettled in rank grease,
grainy images of haytime

and village shows. Two farm
    women rope a prize cow,
dragging it from that long

gone August day pixilating
    from silver emulsion that
might have purified from

seams of lead. No memory
    there of the Swale path, the
corpse road, melding tongues

with earth and bone – worn
    by water, by boots: dumb
face-downward stone.

Visitation

When we came here I thought I'd
    brought you home with me, back

to the source, back to the split stone
    of our destiny: dark haired, dark-eyed

letting go your old faith to live in stark
    uncertainties. We stayed in that cottage

by the church where an old man in
    tooled boots and a Stetson knocked

one day, his vowels mined from England's
    North, flown back from Texas to the green

Norse fields he couldn't forget. Nineteen-
    thirteen: he'd stayed here then, snared rabbits

on the river flats for the farmer's wife
    to skin into a pie, then sailed far west

to find another life leaving his friends
    to fall to Europe's febrile maw. We

brought him inside and he cried the
    way a child sobs for some unnamed

thing, inconsolably old, come home to
    die at last. He thanked us with blue-veined

hands and when he left we made love
    in that bedroom with its croaking boards

and whitewashed walls, its crooked
    sashes and thinning glass, knowing our

haptic touch was all there was to
    say: our bodies tangled in cool sheets,

your cream-skim skin under my
    tongue; wild rose aureoles, sun's

glittering wedge of dust, the cast
    petticoats of thorn trees on the fell.

Colony Collapse

This ether of honey is clover,
bistort, cranesbill, creeping
    buttercup, the pale frocks
of fool's parsley, thistle heads
    that goldfinches squabble at.

Not one butterfly
alights or honey bee thrums
    in foxgloves, bumbling from
purple bells, pockets
    crammed with pollen.

Their colonies fail –
even pheromones fade
    there – the language for
each flower lost at the
    hive's finger-tight entry.

Those sentries have
found the sleep of lost
    vigilance, its fading drone
of wings: incalculable,
    everlasting dark.

Funerary

The Swale is quick here.
      Once I scrambled out on
wet stones to let my parents
      slip away: peat-brown

water, a long soft syllable
      of ash. Curlews liquefy
damp air, the plaster-lath
      gable of the farm I

dreamed I slept under
      in some former life, burst
to a buttress of spilled
      rubble, distempered

walls, a century's filth.
      At the old workings we
watch a dipper feed one
      fat chick, its screams

teetering on the cusp
      of hunger and self-love;
the chant of water going
      on, its untranslatable

plainsong slaking a day's
      sweet spaciousness.

Quotidian

Riverside sward stinks of
    death's rust: shot rabbits'
eye holes accusing light
    of entry. Now a wagtail
sulphur-breasted,

lambs, panting in thorn
    roots; a day so hot it
twists iron trunks, the chink
    of oystercatchers telling
coin, a sandpiper shy

at its breeding ground.
    Now a buzzard's Calvary
of blazing air, bullocks
    at the water's edge
mooning, white-eyed,

a small boy bending
    over tadpoles in a pool
hermeneutic to their
    scrambled writ. A
warbler darts into

the sedge, cow dung
    daubs a claggy memory,
its recollection reaching
    before words, rich in every
thing felt, everything

unspoken. The day pours
    heat at the valley head,
ascending as ribbed ice
    above the track where
I've seen sparrowhawks

court at dusk, that
        memory singing here
again, the path spurning
        the gill, climbing its own
mirage: pale sand

sifting the hours, a
        white swarm rising.

Reprise

The city turns – daylight to nightglow –
    horizons backlit by its prophecy. Vowels

purr through airwaves jammed with
    ghosts, each jostling voice a new embodiment –

foreign blood mixed with local grit
    to better the aggregate of its long telling.

Here, in this valley's parched
    throat, struck stone smells of war;

those grave slabs face-down make
    pathways of lost bible lore; these flower

heads white as palsied washdays, the bees'
    semiotic fugue quaint as lost madrigals.

All moment and memory lofted here:
    summer hawks courting as self-shadows,

twin consequence, fledged passions
    of air. Blossom laces blackthorn, its

lingering scent of loss, the Swale
    quick as tanned muscle, bee foragers

wayward as words, gathering
    quintessence only to fade, to fail us.

The freight of tongues scribed under
    flat stone, unredeemed, the means of

remembrance forgetting itself: face-
    down, text-down, everlastingly laid

down. And the city turning still, its epic
    yarn spinning a shroud of silence: Earth's

dimming ember sucking at reservoirs
    of coal, oil, shale, at the atom's spilled

seed, its bright, blind, brief occluded
    eye looming in space, fading as stretching

waves of light – what *was* becoming
    what is, will be.

Acknowledgements

The Rialto, The Interpreter's House, Brittle Star, Canto, The North, Acumen, Carillon, Poetry Review, Poetry Society Website, Dream Catcher, The Long Poem Magazine, New Contrast (South Africa), *Poetry Bay* (US), *Poetry* (US), *Tremble* (VC Canberra Prize Anthology 2016).

'Midland Rail' was commissioned for *More Raw Material,* an anthology of work inspired by Alan Sillitoe, Lucifer Press; 'Diablo' was longlisted in the 2015 National Poetry Competition; 'Ordinary' was shortlisted for the 2016 Canberra VC Prize.

Thanks to Chris Stroud and Meg Vandermerwe of the Centre for Multilinguism and Diversity, University of the Western Cape, South Africa, for their hospitality during my six week Fellowship in April/May 2014 which enabled me to write new poems and carry out substantial work on the manuscript of this book.

Many thanks to the artist John Colton for permission to use a detail from his diptych painting of the west face of the Drus on the cover of this book.